50 Cozy Winter Warmth Recipes for Home

By: Kelly Johnson

Table of Contents

- Classic Chicken Noodle Soup
- Beef and Barley Stew
- Creamy Tomato Basil Soup
- Butternut Squash Soup
- Loaded Baked Potato Soup
- Chili con Carne
- French Onion Soup
- Split Pea Soup
- Vegetable Beef Soup
- Creamy Mushroom Soup
- Pumpkin Spice Latte
- Hot Chocolate with Marshmallows
- Mulled Wine
- Spiced Apple Cider
- Cinnamon Roll Casserole
- Baked Macaroni and Cheese
- Cheesy Broccoli Casserole
- Chicken Pot Pie
- Vegetable Curry
- Stuffed Bell Peppers
- Eggplant Parmesan
- Shepherd's Pie
- Gingerbread Cookies
- Slow Cooker Beef Stew
- Pumpkin Bread
- Honey Garlic Glazed Carrots
- Roasted Brussels Sprouts
- Cranberry Sauce
- Apple Crisp
- Chocolate Chip Cookies
- Peanut Butter Hot Chocolate
- Creamy Garlic Mashed Potatoes
- Honey-Balsamic Roasted Vegetables
- Sweet Potato Casserole
- Spinach and Feta Stuffed Shells

- Caramelized Onion and Gruyère Tart
- Lentil Soup
- Potato Leek Soup
- Vegetable Lasagna
- Braised Short Ribs
- Oven-Baked Risotto
- Spaghetti Carbonara
- Savory Pumpkin Soup
- Pork Tenderloin with Apples
- Baked Ziti
- Chocolate Lava Cake
- Pumpkin Spice Muffins
- Warm Quinoa Salad
- Cider-Braised Pork Chops
- Raspberry Crumble Bars

Classic Chicken Noodle Soup

Ingredients

- 1 tablespoon olive oil
- 1 onion, chopped
- 2 carrots, sliced
- 2 celery stalks, sliced
- 3 garlic cloves, minced
- 8 cups chicken broth
- 2 cups cooked chicken, shredded
- 1 teaspoon dried thyme
- 1 bay leaf
- 2 cups egg noodles
- Salt and pepper to taste
- Fresh parsley, chopped (for garnish)

Instructions

1. **Sauté the Vegetables:**
   - In a large pot, heat olive oil over medium heat. Add onion, carrots, and celery. Cook until softened, about 5 minutes.
2. **Add Garlic and Broth:**
   - Stir in garlic, cook for another minute, then add chicken broth, shredded chicken, thyme, and bay leaf. Bring to a boil.
3. **Cook the Noodles:**
   - Add egg noodles and cook according to package instructions until tender. Season with salt and pepper. Remove bay leaf before serving and garnish with parsley.

Beef and Barley Stew

Ingredients

- 2 pounds beef chuck, cut into 1-inch pieces
- 2 tablespoons olive oil
- 1 onion, chopped
- 3 carrots, chopped
- 3 celery stalks, chopped
- 3 garlic cloves, minced
- 6 cups beef broth
- 1 cup pearl barley
- 1 teaspoon dried thyme
- 1 bay leaf
- Salt and pepper to taste

Instructions

1. **Brown the Beef:**
    - In a large pot, heat olive oil over medium-high heat. Add beef and brown on all sides. Remove and set aside.
2. **Sauté Vegetables:**
    - In the same pot, add onion, carrots, and celery. Cook until softened, about 5 minutes. Stir in garlic and cook for another minute.
3. **Combine and Simmer:**
    - Return beef to the pot, add beef broth, barley, thyme, and bay leaf. Bring to a boil, then reduce heat and simmer for 1.5 to 2 hours until beef is tender. Season with salt and pepper before serving.

Creamy Tomato Basil Soup

Ingredients

- 2 tablespoons olive oil
- 1 onion, chopped
- 4 garlic cloves, minced
- 2 cans (28 ounces each) crushed tomatoes
- 1 cup vegetable broth
- 1 teaspoon dried basil
- ½ cup heavy cream
- Salt and pepper to taste
- Fresh basil, for garnish

Instructions

1. **Sauté Onion and Garlic:**
   - In a large pot, heat olive oil over medium heat. Add onion and cook until translucent, about 5 minutes. Stir in garlic and cook for 1 minute.
2. **Add Tomatoes and Broth:**
   - Add crushed tomatoes, vegetable broth, and dried basil. Bring to a simmer and cook for 20 minutes.
3. **Blend and Finish:**
   - Use an immersion blender to purée the soup until smooth. Stir in heavy cream, season with salt and pepper, and serve garnished with fresh basil.

Butternut Squash Soup

Ingredients

- 2 tablespoons olive oil
- 1 onion, chopped
- 2 cloves garlic, minced
- 1 butternut squash, peeled and diced
- 4 cups vegetable broth
- 1 teaspoon ground cinnamon
- Salt and pepper to taste
- ½ cup heavy cream (optional)
- Pumpkin seeds (for garnish)

Instructions

1. **Sauté Onion and Garlic:**
    - In a large pot, heat olive oil over medium heat. Add onion and cook until soft, about 5 minutes. Stir in garlic and cook for another minute.
2. **Add Squash and Broth:**
    - Add diced butternut squash, vegetable broth, and cinnamon. Bring to a boil, then reduce heat and simmer for about 20-25 minutes until squash is tender.
3. **Blend and Serve:**
    - Purée the soup with an immersion blender. If desired, stir in heavy cream. Season with salt and pepper and serve topped with pumpkin seeds.

Loaded Baked Potato Soup

Ingredients

- 4 large russet potatoes, baked and cooled
- 2 tablespoons butter
- 1 onion, chopped
- 3 garlic cloves, minced
- 4 cups chicken or vegetable broth
- 1 cup heavy cream
- 1 cup shredded cheddar cheese
- ½ cup cooked bacon, crumbled
- ¼ cup green onions, chopped
- Salt and pepper to taste

Instructions

1. **Sauté Onion and Garlic:**
   - In a large pot, melt butter over medium heat. Add onion and cook until soft, about 5 minutes. Stir in garlic and cook for another minute.
2. **Add Potatoes and Broth:**
   - Peel and cube the baked potatoes, add to the pot with broth. Bring to a boil, then reduce heat and simmer for 10 minutes.
3. **Finish the Soup:**
   - Stir in heavy cream, cheese, bacon, and green onions. Season with salt and pepper before serving.

Chili con Carne

Ingredients

- 1 tablespoon olive oil
- 1 onion, chopped
- 2 garlic cloves, minced
- 1 pound ground beef
- 1 can (15 ounces) kidney beans, drained and rinsed
- 1 can (15 ounces) black beans, drained and rinsed
- 1 can (28 ounces) crushed tomatoes
- 2 tablespoons chili powder
- 1 teaspoon cumin
- Salt and pepper to taste

Instructions

1. **Sauté Onion and Garlic:**
   - In a large pot, heat olive oil over medium heat. Add onion and cook until soft, about 5 minutes. Stir in garlic and cook for another minute.
2. **Brown the Beef:**
   - Add ground beef to the pot and cook until browned, breaking it apart with a spoon.
3. **Combine Ingredients:**
   - Stir in beans, crushed tomatoes, chili powder, cumin, salt, and pepper. Bring to a simmer and cook for 30 minutes. Serve hot.

French Onion Soup

Ingredients

- 4 tablespoons butter
- 4 large onions, thinly sliced
- 4 cups beef broth
- 1 cup white wine
- 1 teaspoon thyme
- Salt and pepper to taste
- Baguette slices, toasted
- 2 cups Gruyère cheese, grated

Instructions

1. **Caramelize the Onions:**
    - In a large pot, melt butter over medium heat. Add onions and cook slowly, stirring occasionally, until caramelized, about 30 minutes.
2. **Add Broth and Wine:**
    - Pour in beef broth and white wine. Add thyme, salt, and pepper. Bring to a simmer and cook for 20 minutes.
3. **Serve:**
    - Ladle soup into bowls, top with toasted baguette slices, and sprinkle with cheese. Broil until cheese is bubbly and golden.

Split Pea Soup

Ingredients

- 1 tablespoon olive oil
- 1 onion, chopped
- 2 carrots, chopped
- 2 celery stalks, chopped
- 2 garlic cloves, minced
- 1 pound split peas, rinsed
- 6 cups vegetable or chicken broth
- 1 teaspoon thyme
- Salt and pepper to taste
- 1 ham hock (optional)

Instructions

1. **Sauté Vegetables:**
    - In a large pot, heat olive oil over medium heat. Add onion, carrots, and celery. Cook until softened, about 5 minutes. Stir in garlic and cook for another minute.
2. **Combine Ingredients:**
    - Add split peas, broth, thyme, salt, pepper, and ham hock if using. Bring to a boil, then reduce heat and simmer for 1-1.5 hours until peas are tender.
3. **Blend and Serve:**
    - Remove ham hock, shred meat, and return to the soup. Purée if desired for a creamy texture. Adjust seasoning before serving.

Vegetable Beef Soup

Ingredients

- 1 tablespoon olive oil
- 1 pound beef stew meat, cut into cubes
- 1 onion, chopped
- 3 carrots, chopped
- 3 celery stalks, chopped
- 3 garlic cloves, minced
- 8 cups beef broth
- 2 cups mixed vegetables (like peas, corn, and green beans)
- 1 teaspoon dried thyme
- Salt and pepper to taste

Instructions

1. **Brown the Beef:**
    - In a large pot, heat olive oil over medium heat. Add beef and brown on all sides. Remove and set aside.
2. **Sauté Vegetables:**
    - In the same pot, add onion, carrots, and celery. Cook until softened, about 5 minutes. Stir in garlic and cook for another minute.
3. **Combine and Simmer:**
    - Return beef to the pot, add broth, mixed vegetables, thyme, salt, and pepper. Bring to a boil, then reduce heat and simmer for 1-1.5 hours until beef is tender. Adjust seasoning before serving.

Creamy Mushroom Soup

Ingredients

- 2 tablespoons butter
- 1 onion, chopped
- 3 garlic cloves, minced
- 16 ounces mushrooms, sliced
- 4 cups vegetable or chicken broth
- 1 cup heavy cream
- 1 teaspoon thyme
- Salt and pepper to taste
- Fresh parsley, chopped (for garnish)

Instructions

1. **Sauté the Onions and Garlic:**
    - In a large pot, melt butter over medium heat. Add onion and cook until translucent, about 5 minutes. Stir in garlic and cook for another minute.
2. **Cook the Mushrooms:**
    - Add sliced mushrooms to the pot and cook until softened and browned, about 10 minutes.
3. **Add Broth and Blend:**
    - Pour in the broth and thyme. Bring to a simmer and cook for 15 minutes. Use an immersion blender to purée the soup until smooth. Stir in heavy cream, season with salt and pepper, and serve garnished with parsley.

Pumpkin Spice Latte

Ingredients

- 2 cups milk (or non-dairy alternative)
- 2 tablespoons pumpkin puree
- 2 tablespoons sugar
- 1 teaspoon pumpkin pie spice
- 1 teaspoon vanilla extract
- 1 shot espresso (or ¼ cup strong coffee)
- Whipped cream (for topping)
- Extra pumpkin pie spice (for garnish)

Instructions

1. **Heat the Milk:**
   - In a saucepan over medium heat, whisk together milk, pumpkin puree, sugar, pumpkin pie spice, and vanilla until heated through but not boiling.
2. **Combine with Coffee:**
   - Brew espresso or strong coffee. Pour into a large mug and add the heated milk mixture. Stir to combine.
3. **Serve:**
   - Top with whipped cream and a sprinkle of pumpkin pie spice. Enjoy warm.

Hot Chocolate with Marshmallows

Ingredients

- 2 cups milk (or non-dairy alternative)
- 2 tablespoons unsweetened cocoa powder
- 2 tablespoons sugar
- 1 teaspoon vanilla extract
- Pinch of salt
- Mini marshmallows (for topping)

Instructions

1. **Heat the Milk:**
    - In a saucepan over medium heat, warm the milk until hot but not boiling.
2. **Mix the Cocoa:**
    - In a small bowl, whisk together cocoa powder, sugar, and salt. Gradually add a few tablespoons of the hot milk to the dry mixture to create a smooth paste.
3. **Combine and Serve:**
    - Stir the cocoa paste back into the saucepan with the remaining milk and add vanilla. Heat until hot, then pour into mugs and top with mini marshmallows.

Mulled Wine

Ingredients

- 1 bottle (750 ml) red wine
- 1 orange, sliced
- 1 apple, sliced
- 2 cinnamon sticks
- 5 whole cloves
- 3 star anise
- ¼ cup honey (or to taste)

Instructions

1. **Combine Ingredients:**
    - In a large pot, combine red wine, orange slices, apple slices, cinnamon sticks, cloves, star anise, and honey.
2. **Simmer:**
    - Heat over low heat until warm but not boiling. Let simmer for about 20-30 minutes to allow the flavors to meld.
3. **Serve:**
    - Strain the mixture and serve warm in mugs.

Spiced Apple Cider

Ingredients

- 4 cups apple cider
- 1 orange, sliced
- 2 cinnamon sticks
- 5 whole cloves
- 1 teaspoon allspice
- 1 tablespoon brown sugar (optional)

Instructions

1. **Combine Ingredients:**
    - In a large pot, combine apple cider, orange slices, cinnamon sticks, cloves, allspice, and brown sugar (if using).
2. **Simmer:**
    - Heat over medium heat until hot but not boiling. Let simmer for 15-20 minutes to infuse the flavors.
3. **Serve:**
    - Strain the cider into mugs and enjoy warm.

Cinnamon Roll Casserole

Ingredients

- 2 cans refrigerated cinnamon rolls
- 4 large eggs
- 1 cup milk
- 1 teaspoon vanilla extract
- 1 teaspoon ground cinnamon
- ½ cup maple syrup (for drizzling)

Instructions

1. **Preheat Oven:**
    - Preheat oven to 350°F (175°C).
2. **Prepare the Cinnamon Rolls:**
    - Cut the cinnamon rolls into quarters and place them in a greased 9x13-inch baking dish.
3. **Mix the Egg Mixture:**
    - In a bowl, whisk together eggs, milk, vanilla extract, and ground cinnamon. Pour over the cinnamon rolls.
4. **Bake:**
    - Bake for 25-30 minutes or until the center is set. Drizzle with maple syrup before serving.

Baked Macaroni and Cheese

Ingredients

- 2 cups elbow macaroni
- 2 tablespoons butter
- 2 tablespoons all-purpose flour
- 2 cups milk
- 2 cups shredded cheddar cheese
- 1 teaspoon mustard powder
- Salt and pepper to taste
- ½ cup breadcrumbs (optional, for topping)

Instructions

1. **Cook the Pasta:**
   - Cook macaroni according to package instructions. Drain and set aside.
2. **Make the Cheese Sauce:**
   - In a large pot, melt butter over medium heat. Stir in flour and cook for 1 minute. Gradually add milk, whisking until smooth and thickened. Remove from heat and stir in cheese, mustard powder, salt, and pepper.
3. **Combine and Bake:**
   - Stir cooked macaroni into the cheese sauce. Pour into a greased baking dish. If desired, sprinkle breadcrumbs on top. Bake at 350°F (175°C) for 20-25 minutes until bubbly and golden.

Cheesy Broccoli Casserole

Ingredients

- 4 cups broccoli florets, steamed
- 1 cup cooked rice
- 1 cup shredded cheddar cheese
- 1 can (10.5 ounces) cream of mushroom soup
- ½ cup milk
- ½ teaspoon garlic powder
- Salt and pepper to taste
- ½ cup breadcrumbs (optional, for topping)

Instructions

1. **Preheat Oven:**
   - Preheat oven to 350°F (175°C).
2. **Mix Ingredients:**
   - In a large bowl, combine steamed broccoli, cooked rice, ½ cup cheese, cream of mushroom soup, milk, garlic powder, salt, and pepper. Mix well.
3. **Transfer and Bake:**
   - Pour mixture into a greased baking dish. Sprinkle with remaining cheese and breadcrumbs if using. Bake for 25-30 minutes until hot and bubbly.

Chicken Pot Pie

Ingredients

- 1 pound cooked chicken, shredded
- 1 cup frozen peas and carrots
- 1 cup frozen corn
- 1/3 cup butter
- 1/3 cup all-purpose flour
- 1 ¾ cups chicken broth
- 2/3 cup milk
- 1 teaspoon salt
- 1 teaspoon black pepper
- 1 teaspoon dried thyme
- 1 package refrigerated pie crusts (2 crusts)

Instructions

1. **Preheat Oven:**
   - Preheat the oven to 425°F (220°C).
2. **Prepare Filling:**
   - In a large saucepan, melt butter over medium heat. Stir in flour and cook for 1-2 minutes until bubbly. Gradually add chicken broth and milk, stirring until thickened. Add chicken, peas, corn, salt, pepper, and thyme.
3. **Assemble Pie:**
   - Place one pie crust in a 9-inch pie pan. Pour the filling into the crust and cover with the second crust. Cut slits in the top to allow steam to escape.
4. **Bake:**
   - Bake for 30-35 minutes until golden brown. Let cool for a few minutes before serving.

Vegetable Curry

Ingredients

- 2 tablespoons oil
- 1 onion, chopped
- 2 garlic cloves, minced
- 1 tablespoon ginger, grated
- 1 tablespoon curry powder
- 1 can (14 ounces) coconut milk
- 2 cups mixed vegetables (carrots, bell peppers, peas, etc.)
- 1 can (14 ounces) chickpeas, drained and rinsed
- Salt to taste
- Fresh cilantro (for garnish)

Instructions

1. **Sauté Aromatics:**
    - In a large pot, heat oil over medium heat. Add onion and cook until soft, about 5 minutes. Stir in garlic and ginger, cooking for another minute.
2. **Add Spices and Vegetables:**
    - Add curry powder, stir well, then pour in coconut milk. Add mixed vegetables and chickpeas. Simmer for 15-20 minutes until vegetables are tender.
3. **Season and Serve:**
    - Season with salt to taste and garnish with fresh cilantro before serving. Serve hot with rice or naan.

Stuffed Bell Peppers

Ingredients

- 4 large bell peppers, tops cut off and seeds removed
- 1 pound ground beef (or turkey)
- 1 cup cooked rice
- 1 can (14 ounces) diced tomatoes
- 1 teaspoon Italian seasoning
- Salt and pepper to taste
- 1 cup shredded cheese (optional)

Instructions

1. **Preheat Oven:**
   - Preheat oven to 375°F (190°C).
2. **Prepare Filling:**
   - In a skillet, cook ground beef over medium heat until browned. Drain excess fat. Stir in cooked rice, diced tomatoes, Italian seasoning, salt, and pepper.
3. **Stuff Peppers:**
   - Place bell peppers in a baking dish. Fill each pepper with the meat mixture. If desired, sprinkle cheese on top.
4. **Bake:**
   - Cover with foil and bake for 25-30 minutes. Remove foil and bake for an additional 10 minutes until peppers are tender.

Eggplant Parmesan

Ingredients

- 2 medium eggplants, sliced into rounds
- 2 cups marinara sauce
- 2 cups shredded mozzarella cheese
- 1 cup grated Parmesan cheese
- 1 cup breadcrumbs
- 2 eggs, beaten
- Salt and pepper to taste
- Olive oil (for frying)

Instructions

1. **Preheat Oven:**
   - Preheat oven to 375°F (190°C).
2. **Prepare Eggplant:**
   - Salt the eggplant slices and let them sit for 30 minutes to draw out moisture. Rinse and pat dry.
3. **Fry Eggplant:**
   - In a skillet, heat olive oil over medium heat. Dip eggplant slices in beaten eggs, then coat with breadcrumbs. Fry until golden on both sides.
4. **Assemble and Bake:**
   - In a baking dish, layer marinara sauce, fried eggplant, mozzarella, and Parmesan. Repeat layers, finishing with cheese on top. Bake for 30-35 minutes until bubbly.

Shepherd's Pie

Ingredients

- 1 pound ground lamb (or beef)
- 1 onion, chopped
- 2 carrots, diced
- 1 cup peas
- 2 tablespoons tomato paste
- 1 cup beef broth
- 4 cups mashed potatoes
- Salt and pepper to taste
- 1 teaspoon Worcestershire sauce

Instructions

1. **Preheat Oven:**
   - Preheat oven to 400°F (200°C).
2. **Cook Filling:**
   - In a skillet, brown the ground meat with onions and carrots until tender. Stir in tomato paste, beef broth, Worcestershire sauce, salt, and pepper. Cook for 5-7 minutes.
3. **Assemble Pie:**
   - Spread the meat mixture in a baking dish and top with peas. Spread mashed potatoes over the top, smoothing it out.
4. **Bake:**
   - Bake for 20-25 minutes until the potatoes are golden. Let cool for a few minutes before serving.

Gingerbread Cookies

Ingredients

- 3 cups all-purpose flour
- 1 teaspoon baking soda
- 1 tablespoon ground ginger
- 1 tablespoon ground cinnamon
- ½ teaspoon ground cloves
- ½ teaspoon salt
- ¾ cup butter, softened
- ¾ cup brown sugar
- 1 large egg
- ½ cup molasses

Instructions

1. **Preheat Oven:**
   - Preheat oven to 350°F (175°C).
2. **Mix Dry Ingredients:**
   - In a bowl, whisk together flour, baking soda, ginger, cinnamon, cloves, and salt.
3. **Cream Butter and Sugar:**
   - In a separate bowl, beat butter and brown sugar until fluffy. Add egg and molasses, mixing until combined.
4. **Combine and Roll:**
   - Gradually add the dry ingredients to the wet mixture. Roll out the dough and cut into shapes.
5. **Bake:**
   - Place on a baking sheet and bake for 8-10 minutes. Let cool before decorating.

Slow Cooker Beef Stew

Ingredients

- 2 pounds beef stew meat, cut into chunks
- 4 cups beef broth
- 4 carrots, sliced
- 3 potatoes, diced
- 1 onion, chopped
- 2 cloves garlic, minced
- 1 teaspoon thyme
- 1 teaspoon salt
- ½ teaspoon pepper

Instructions

1. **Prepare Ingredients:**
   - In a slow cooker, combine beef, broth, carrots, potatoes, onion, garlic, thyme, salt, and pepper.
2. **Cook:**
   - Cover and cook on low for 8 hours or high for 4 hours until the meat is tender. Stir before serving.

Pumpkin Bread

Ingredients

- 1 ½ cups pumpkin puree
- 1 cup sugar
- ½ cup vegetable oil
- 2 large eggs
- 2 cups all-purpose flour
- 1 teaspoon baking soda
- ½ teaspoon baking powder
- 1 teaspoon cinnamon
- ½ teaspoon nutmeg
- ½ teaspoon salt

Instructions

1. **Preheat Oven:**
   - Preheat oven to 350°F (175°C). Grease a loaf pan.
2. **Mix Wet Ingredients:**
   - In a bowl, mix pumpkin puree, sugar, oil, and eggs until smooth.
3. **Combine Dry Ingredients:**
   - In another bowl, whisk together flour, baking soda, baking powder, cinnamon, nutmeg, and salt. Gradually add to the wet mixture.
4. **Bake:**
   - Pour batter into the prepared loaf pan and bake for 60-70 minutes until a toothpick comes out clean. Let cool before slicing.

Honey Garlic Glazed Carrots

Ingredients

- 1 pound baby carrots
- 2 tablespoons honey
- 2 tablespoons butter
- 2 cloves garlic, minced
- Salt and pepper to taste
- Fresh parsley (for garnish)

Instructions

1. **Prepare Carrots:**
    - In a large pot, bring water to a boil. Add the baby carrots and cook for 5-7 minutes until tender. Drain.
2. **Make Glaze:**
    - In a skillet, melt butter over medium heat. Add garlic and sauté for 1 minute. Stir in honey, salt, and pepper.
3. **Glaze Carrots:**
    - Add the cooked carrots to the skillet, tossing to coat in the honey garlic mixture. Cook for another 2-3 minutes until heated through.
4. **Serve:**
    - Garnish with fresh parsley before serving.

Roasted Brussels Sprouts

Ingredients

- 1 pound Brussels sprouts, halved
- 3 tablespoons olive oil
- Salt and pepper to taste
- 1 tablespoon balsamic vinegar (optional)
- Parmesan cheese (optional)

Instructions

1. **Preheat Oven:**
    - Preheat oven to 400°F (200°C).
2. **Prepare Sprouts:**
    - In a bowl, toss halved Brussels sprouts with olive oil, salt, and pepper until well coated.
3. **Roast:**
    - Spread the Brussels sprouts on a baking sheet in a single layer. Roast for 20-25 minutes until golden brown and crispy, stirring halfway through.
4. **Finish:**
    - Drizzle with balsamic vinegar and sprinkle with Parmesan cheese before serving, if desired.

Cranberry Sauce

Ingredients

- 12 ounces fresh cranberries
- 1 cup sugar
- 1 cup water
- Zest of 1 orange (optional)
- 1 cinnamon stick (optional)

Instructions

1. **Cook Cranberries:**
   - In a saucepan, combine cranberries, sugar, and water. Bring to a boil over medium heat.
2. **Simmer:**
   - Reduce heat and simmer for 10-15 minutes until cranberries burst and the sauce thickens. Stir in orange zest and cinnamon stick if using.
3. **Cool:**
   - Remove from heat and let cool. The sauce will thicken as it cools. Serve chilled or at room temperature.

Apple Crisp

Ingredients

- 6 cups sliced apples (about 6 medium apples)
- 1 cup brown sugar
- 1 cup rolled oats
- 1 cup all-purpose flour
- 1 teaspoon cinnamon
- ½ cup butter, softened
- 1 teaspoon vanilla extract (optional)

Instructions

1. **Preheat Oven:**
   - Preheat oven to 350°F (175°C). Grease a baking dish.
2. **Prepare Filling:**
   - Place sliced apples in the baking dish. Sprinkle with ½ cup brown sugar and cinnamon.
3. **Make Topping:**
   - In a bowl, mix oats, flour, remaining brown sugar, and softened butter until crumbly. Add vanilla extract if desired.
4. **Assemble and Bake:**
   - Spread the topping over the apples. Bake for 30-35 minutes until golden brown and apples are tender. Serve warm, optionally with ice cream.

Chocolate Chip Cookies

Ingredients

- 1 cup butter, softened
- 1 cup granulated sugar
- 1 cup brown sugar, packed
- 2 large eggs
- 2 teaspoons vanilla extract
- 3 cups all-purpose flour
- 1 teaspoon baking soda
- ½ teaspoon salt
- 2 cups chocolate chips

Instructions

1. **Preheat Oven:**
    - Preheat oven to 350°F (175°C). Line baking sheets with parchment paper.
2. **Cream Butter and Sugars:**
    - In a bowl, cream together butter, granulated sugar, and brown sugar until smooth. Beat in eggs and vanilla.
3. **Mix Dry Ingredients:**
    - In another bowl, combine flour, baking soda, and salt. Gradually mix into the wet ingredients. Stir in chocolate chips.
4. **Bake:**
    - Drop rounded tablespoons of dough onto prepared baking sheets. Bake for 10-12 minutes until edges are golden. Let cool before transferring to a wire rack.

Peanut Butter Hot Chocolate

Ingredients

- 2 cups milk
- 2 tablespoons cocoa powder
- 2 tablespoons sugar
- 2 tablespoons creamy peanut butter
- ½ teaspoon vanilla extract
- Whipped cream (for topping)

Instructions

1. **Heat Milk:**
   - In a saucepan, heat milk over medium heat until warm but not boiling.
2. **Mix Cocoa and Sugar:**
   - In a small bowl, whisk together cocoa powder and sugar. Gradually add a few tablespoons of warm milk to create a smooth paste.
3. **Combine Ingredients:**
   - Stir the cocoa mixture back into the saucepan with the remaining milk. Add peanut butter and vanilla, stirring until well combined and heated through.
4. **Serve:**
   - Pour into mugs and top with whipped cream. Enjoy warm.

Creamy Garlic Mashed Potatoes

Ingredients

- 2 pounds potatoes, peeled and cubed
- 4 cloves garlic, minced
- ½ cup sour cream
- ½ cup milk
- 4 tablespoons butter
- Salt and pepper to taste

Instructions

1. **Cook Potatoes:**
    - In a large pot, bring potatoes to a boil in salted water. Cook until tender, about 15-20 minutes. Drain.
2. **Mash Potatoes:**
    - In the same pot, add garlic, sour cream, milk, and butter. Mash until creamy and smooth. Season with salt and pepper to taste.
3. **Serve:**
    - Transfer to a serving dish and garnish with additional butter or herbs, if desired.

Honey-Balsamic Roasted Vegetables

Ingredients

- 2 cups mixed vegetables (carrots, bell peppers, zucchini, etc.)
- 2 tablespoons olive oil
- 1 tablespoon honey
- 1 tablespoon balsamic vinegar
- Salt and pepper to taste

Instructions

1. **Preheat Oven:**
    - Preheat oven to 425°F (220°C).
2. **Prepare Vegetables:**
    - In a bowl, toss mixed vegetables with olive oil, honey, balsamic vinegar, salt, and pepper.
3. **Roast:**
    - Spread vegetables on a baking sheet in a single layer. Roast for 20-25 minutes until tender and caramelized, stirring halfway through.
4. **Serve:**
    - Enjoy warm as a side dish.

Sweet Potato Casserole

Ingredients

- 4 cups mashed sweet potatoes (about 4 medium sweet potatoes)
- ½ cup brown sugar
- ½ cup milk
- 2 eggs
- 1 teaspoon vanilla extract
- ½ teaspoon cinnamon
- 1 cup mini marshmallows (optional)
- ½ cup chopped pecans (optional)

Instructions

1. **Preheat Oven:**
   - Preheat oven to 350°F (175°C). Grease a baking dish.
2. **Prepare Sweet Potato Mixture:**
   - In a bowl, mix mashed sweet potatoes, brown sugar, milk, eggs, vanilla, and cinnamon until smooth. Pour into the prepared baking dish.
3. **Top and Bake:**
   - If desired, sprinkle marshmallows and pecans on top. Bake for 30-35 minutes until heated through and marshmallows are golden.
4. **Serve:**
   - Enjoy warm as a side dish or dessert.

Spinach and Feta Stuffed Shells

Ingredients

- 12 jumbo pasta shells
- 1 cup ricotta cheese
- 1 cup fresh spinach, chopped
- ½ cup feta cheese, crumbled
- 1 cup marinara sauce
- 1 cup mozzarella cheese, shredded
- 1 egg
- 1 teaspoon garlic powder
- Salt and pepper to taste
- Fresh basil (for garnish)

Instructions

1. **Preheat Oven:**
   - Preheat oven to 375°F (190°C). Cook the jumbo shells according to package instructions until al dente. Drain and set aside.
2. **Prepare Filling:**
   - In a bowl, mix ricotta, chopped spinach, feta, egg, garlic powder, salt, and pepper until well combined.
3. **Stuff Shells:**
   - Spread ½ cup of marinara sauce on the bottom of a baking dish. Fill each shell with the cheese mixture and place in the dish. Pour remaining marinara sauce over the shells and top with mozzarella cheese.
4. **Bake:**
   - Cover with foil and bake for 20 minutes. Remove foil and bake for an additional 10 minutes until cheese is bubbly and golden. Garnish with fresh basil before serving.

Caramelized Onion and Gruyère Tart

Ingredients

- 1 sheet puff pastry, thawed
- 2 large onions, thinly sliced
- 2 tablespoons olive oil
- 1 teaspoon sugar
- 1 cup Gruyère cheese, shredded
- 2 eggs
- ½ cup heavy cream
- Salt and pepper to taste
- Fresh thyme (for garnish)

Instructions

1. **Preheat Oven:**
    - Preheat oven to 400°F (200°C). Roll out the puff pastry and fit it into a tart pan. Prick the bottom with a fork.
2. **Caramelize Onions:**
    - In a skillet, heat olive oil over medium heat. Add sliced onions and sugar, cooking until caramelized, about 20 minutes. Season with salt and pepper.
3. **Assemble Tart:**
    - Spread caramelized onions evenly over the pastry. Sprinkle Gruyère cheese on top. In a bowl, whisk together eggs, heavy cream, salt, and pepper. Pour over the tart.
4. **Bake:**
    - Bake for 25-30 minutes until set and golden brown. Garnish with fresh thyme before serving.

Lentil Soup

Ingredients

- 1 cup lentils, rinsed
- 1 onion, diced
- 2 carrots, diced
- 2 celery stalks, diced
- 3 cloves garlic, minced
- 6 cups vegetable broth
- 1 teaspoon cumin
- 1 teaspoon thyme
- Salt and pepper to taste
- Olive oil for sautéing

Instructions

1. **Sauté Vegetables:**
     - In a large pot, heat olive oil over medium heat. Add onion, carrots, and celery, sautéing until softened, about 5-7 minutes. Stir in garlic and cook for an additional minute.
2. **Add Lentils and Spices:**
     - Add lentils, vegetable broth, cumin, thyme, salt, and pepper. Bring to a boil, then reduce heat and simmer for 30-35 minutes until lentils are tender.
3. **Blend (Optional):**
     - For a smoother texture, blend part of the soup with an immersion blender. Adjust seasoning as needed before serving.

Potato Leek Soup

Ingredients

- 3 leeks, cleaned and sliced
- 4 large potatoes, peeled and diced
- 1 onion, diced
- 4 cups vegetable broth
- 1 cup heavy cream
- Salt and pepper to taste
- Olive oil for sautéing

Instructions

1. **Sauté Leeks and Onion:**
   - In a large pot, heat olive oil over medium heat. Add leeks and onion, sautéing until softened, about 5 minutes.
2. **Add Potatoes and Broth:**
   - Add diced potatoes and vegetable broth. Bring to a boil, then reduce heat and simmer for 20-25 minutes until potatoes are tender.
3. **Blend and Finish:**
   - Use an immersion blender to puree the soup until smooth. Stir in heavy cream and season with salt and pepper before serving.

Vegetable Lasagna

Ingredients

- 9 lasagna noodles
- 2 cups marinara sauce
- 2 cups ricotta cheese
- 2 cups spinach, chopped
- 1 zucchini, thinly sliced
- 1 bell pepper, diced
- 1 cup mozzarella cheese, shredded
- 1 teaspoon Italian seasoning
- Salt and pepper to taste

Instructions

1. **Preheat Oven:**
    - Preheat oven to 375°F (190°C). Cook lasagna noodles according to package instructions. Drain and set aside.
2. **Layer Ingredients:**
    - In a baking dish, spread a layer of marinara sauce. Place 3 noodles on top. Spread half of the ricotta, half of the spinach, zucchini, and bell pepper. Sprinkle with Italian seasoning, salt, and pepper. Repeat layers, ending with noodles and marinara sauce on top.
3. **Top and Bake:**
    - Top with mozzarella cheese. Cover with foil and bake for 30 minutes. Remove foil and bake for an additional 10-15 minutes until cheese is bubbly and golden. Let cool slightly before serving.

Braised Short Ribs

Ingredients

- 3 pounds beef short ribs
- 2 tablespoons olive oil
- 1 onion, diced
- 2 carrots, diced
- 2 cloves garlic, minced
- 2 cups red wine
- 4 cups beef broth
- 1 tablespoon thyme
- Salt and pepper to taste

Instructions

1. **Brown Ribs:**
   - In a large Dutch oven, heat olive oil over medium-high heat. Season short ribs with salt and pepper. Brown the ribs on all sides, then remove and set aside.
2. **Sauté Vegetables:**
   - In the same pot, add onion, carrots, and garlic. Sauté until softened, about 5 minutes.
3. **Deglaze and Braise:**
   - Pour in red wine, scraping up browned bits. Return short ribs to the pot, add beef broth and thyme. Bring to a boil, then reduce heat to low and cover. Simmer for 2-3 hours until tender.
4. **Serve:**
   - Serve ribs with the cooking liquid spooned over them.

Oven-Baked Risotto

Ingredients

- 1 cup Arborio rice
- 4 cups vegetable or chicken broth
- 1 onion, diced
- 2 cloves garlic, minced
- 1 cup peas (fresh or frozen)
- 1 cup Parmesan cheese, grated
- 2 tablespoons olive oil
- Salt and pepper to taste
- Fresh parsley (for garnish)

Instructions

1. **Preheat Oven:**
    - Preheat oven to 375°F (190°C).
2. **Sauté Aromatics:**
    - In an oven-safe pot, heat olive oil over medium heat. Add onion and garlic, sautéing until softened, about 5 minutes.
3. **Add Rice:**
    - Stir in Arborio rice, cooking for 1-2 minutes. Add broth and bring to a boil.
4. **Bake:**
    - Cover the pot and transfer it to the oven. Bake for 25 minutes. Remove and stir in peas and Parmesan cheese. Adjust seasoning before serving and garnish with fresh parsley.

Spaghetti Carbonara

Ingredients

- 12 ounces spaghetti
- 4 ounces pancetta or bacon, diced
- 2 large eggs
- 1 cup Parmesan cheese, grated
- 2 cloves garlic, minced
- Salt and black pepper to taste
- Fresh parsley (for garnish)

Instructions

1. **Cook Spaghetti:**
   - In a large pot, cook spaghetti according to package instructions. Reserve 1 cup of pasta water and drain the rest.
2. **Cook Pancetta:**
   - In a skillet, cook pancetta or bacon over medium heat until crispy. Add garlic and cook for an additional minute.
3. **Mix Eggs and Cheese:**
   - In a bowl, whisk together eggs, Parmesan cheese, salt, and black pepper.
4. **Combine and Serve:**
   - Add hot pasta to the skillet with pancetta. Remove from heat, then quickly mix in the egg mixture, adding reserved pasta water as needed to create a creamy sauce. Serve immediately, garnished with parsley.

Savory Pumpkin Soup

Ingredients

- 2 cups pumpkin puree (canned or fresh)
- 1 onion, diced
- 2 cloves garlic, minced
- 4 cups vegetable broth
- 1 teaspoon cumin
- 1 teaspoon cinnamon
- ½ cup coconut milk
- Salt and pepper to taste
- Olive oil for sautéing

Instructions

1. **Sauté Onion and Garlic:**
   - In a pot, heat olive oil over medium heat. Add onion and garlic, sautéing until softened, about 5 minutes.
2. **Add Pumpkin and Spices:**
   - Stir in pumpkin puree, vegetable broth, cumin, and cinnamon. Bring to a boil, then reduce heat and simmer for 15-20 minutes.
3. **Blend and Finish:**
   - Use an immersion blender to puree the soup until smooth. Stir in coconut milk and season with salt and pepper before serving.

Pork Tenderloin with Apples

Ingredients

- 1.5 pounds pork tenderloin
- 2 tablespoons olive oil
- Salt and pepper to taste
- 2 apples, sliced (preferably Granny Smith)
- 1 onion, sliced
- 1 cup apple cider
- 1 teaspoon thyme
- 1 tablespoon Dijon mustard

Instructions

1. **Preheat Oven:**
   - Preheat your oven to 400°F (200°C).
2. **Season Pork:**
   - Rub the pork tenderloin with olive oil, salt, and pepper. Sear in a hot skillet over medium-high heat until browned on all sides, about 5-7 minutes.
3. **Prepare Apples and Onions:**
   - In the same skillet, add sliced apples and onions. Cook until slightly softened, about 3-4 minutes.
4. **Combine and Roast:**
   - Add apple cider, thyme, and Dijon mustard. Return the pork to the skillet, then transfer everything to the oven. Roast for 20-25 minutes until the pork reaches an internal temperature of 145°F (63°C). Let rest before slicing.

Baked Ziti

Ingredients

- 12 ounces ziti pasta
- 1 jar (24 ounces) marinara sauce
- 2 cups ricotta cheese
- 2 cups mozzarella cheese, shredded
- ½ cup Parmesan cheese, grated
- 1 egg
- 1 teaspoon Italian seasoning
- Salt and pepper to taste
- Fresh basil (for garnish)

Instructions

1. **Preheat Oven:**
   - Preheat oven to 375°F (190°C). Cook ziti pasta according to package instructions until al dente. Drain and set aside.
2. **Mix Ingredients:**
   - In a bowl, mix ricotta cheese, egg, Italian seasoning, salt, and pepper. In a baking dish, combine cooked pasta, marinara sauce, and ricotta mixture. Stir until well combined.
3. **Layer with Cheese:**
   - Top with mozzarella and Parmesan cheese.
4. **Bake:**
   - Cover with foil and bake for 25 minutes. Remove foil and bake for an additional 10-15 minutes until cheese is bubbly and golden. Garnish with fresh basil before serving.

Chocolate Lava Cake

Ingredients

- 1 cup semi-sweet chocolate chips
- ½ cup unsalted butter
- 1 cup powdered sugar
- 2 large eggs
- 2 large egg yolks
- 1 teaspoon vanilla extract
- ½ cup all-purpose flour
- Pinch of salt

Instructions

1. **Preheat Oven:**
    - Preheat oven to 425°F (220°C). Grease four ramekins and place them on a baking sheet.
2. **Melt Chocolate and Butter:**
    - In a microwave-safe bowl, melt chocolate chips and butter together until smooth. Stir in powdered sugar.
3. **Add Eggs and Flour:**
    - Whisk in eggs and egg yolks until combined. Stir in vanilla, flour, and salt until just combined.
4. **Bake:**
    - Divide the batter among the ramekins. Bake for 12-14 minutes until the edges are firm but the center is soft. Let cool for 1 minute, then invert onto plates. Serve warm.

Pumpkin Spice Muffins

Ingredients

- 1 cup pumpkin puree
- ½ cup vegetable oil
- 1 cup sugar
- 2 large eggs
- 1 teaspoon vanilla extract
- 1 ½ cups all-purpose flour
- 1 teaspoon baking soda
- 1 teaspoon baking powder
- 1 teaspoon pumpkin pie spice
- ½ teaspoon salt

Instructions

1. **Preheat Oven:**
   - Preheat oven to 350°F (175°C). Line a muffin tin with paper liners.
2. **Mix Wet Ingredients:**
   - In a large bowl, whisk together pumpkin puree, vegetable oil, sugar, eggs, and vanilla until smooth.
3. **Combine Dry Ingredients:**
   - In another bowl, mix flour, baking soda, baking powder, pumpkin pie spice, and salt. Gradually add to the wet ingredients, stirring until just combined.
4. **Bake:**
   - Fill each muffin cup about two-thirds full. Bake for 20-25 minutes until a toothpick inserted in the center comes out clean. Let cool before serving.

Warm Quinoa Salad

Ingredients

- 1 cup quinoa, rinsed
- 2 cups vegetable broth
- 1 bell pepper, diced
- 1 cup cherry tomatoes, halved
- ½ cup red onion, diced
- 1 cup spinach, chopped
- 2 tablespoons olive oil
- 1 tablespoon lemon juice
- Salt and pepper to taste

Instructions

1. **Cook Quinoa:**
    - In a saucepan, combine quinoa and vegetable broth. Bring to a boil, then reduce heat and simmer for 15 minutes until quinoa is fluffy. Fluff with a fork and let cool slightly.
2. **Mix Salad Ingredients:**
    - In a large bowl, combine cooked quinoa, bell pepper, cherry tomatoes, red onion, and spinach.
3. **Dress Salad:**
    - Drizzle with olive oil and lemon juice. Season with salt and pepper, then toss to combine before serving.

Cider-Braised Pork Chops

Ingredients

- 4 bone-in pork chops
- 2 tablespoons olive oil
- Salt and pepper to taste
- 1 onion, sliced
- 2 apples, sliced
- 1 cup apple cider
- 1 teaspoon thyme
- 1 tablespoon Dijon mustard

Instructions

1. **Sear Pork Chops:**
   - In a large skillet, heat olive oil over medium-high heat. Season pork chops with salt and pepper. Sear on both sides until browned, about 3-4 minutes per side. Remove and set aside.
2. **Sauté Onions and Apples:**
   - In the same skillet, add onion and apples. Sauté until softened, about 5 minutes.
3. **Add Cider and Braise:**
   - Return pork chops to the skillet, add apple cider, thyme, and Dijon mustard. Bring to a simmer, then cover and reduce heat. Cook for 20-25 minutes until pork is tender. Serve with the apple-onion mixture.

Raspberry Crumble Bars

Ingredients

- 1 cup all-purpose flour
- ½ cup rolled oats
- ½ cup brown sugar
- ½ teaspoon baking powder
- ¼ teaspoon salt
- ½ cup unsalted butter, melted
- 1 cup raspberry jam
- ½ cup fresh raspberries (optional)

Instructions

1. **Preheat Oven:**
   - Preheat oven to 350°F (175°C). Grease an 8x8 inch baking dish.
2. **Prepare Crust:**
   - In a bowl, mix flour, oats, brown sugar, baking powder, and salt. Stir in melted butter until crumbly.
3. **Layer Ingredients:**
   - Press half of the mixture into the bottom of the prepared baking dish. Spread raspberry jam evenly on top, then sprinkle with fresh raspberries if using. Crumble remaining mixture over the top.
4. **Bake:**
   - Bake for 25-30 minutes until golden brown. Allow to cool before cutting into bars.